The Southern Writers Quiz Book

UNIVERSITY PRESS OF MISSISSIPPI / JACKSON

THE
Southern Writers
QUIZ BOOK

Patti Carr Black

Illustrations by Patti Henson

http://www.upress.state.ms.us

Copyright © 1999 by University Press of Mississippi
All rights reserved
Manufactured in the United States of America

02 01 00 99   4 3 2 1

The paper in this book meets the guidelines for permanence
and durability of the Committee on Production Guidelines
for Book Longevity of the Council on Library Resources.

Library of Congress Cataloging-in-Publication Data

Black, Patti Carr.
    The southern writers quiz book / Patti Carr Black : illus-
trations by Patti Henson.
        p. cm.
    "A Muscadine book."
    ISBN 1-57806-149-0 (pbk. : alk. paper)
    1. American literature–Southern States–Examinations,
questions,etc. 2. Southern States–Intellectual
life–Examinations, questions, etc. 3. Southern States–In literature–Examinations, questions, etc.   I. Title.
  PS261.B53   1999
  810.9'975–dc21   98-48346
                                                   CIP

British Library Cataloging-in-Publication Data available

Preface

The comment by H. L. Mencken in 1917 that the South was "almost as sterile artistically, intellectually and culturally as the Sahara Desert" set off a reaction that is still reverberating. In 1921, a literary group in New Orleans put out a magazine entitled *The Double Dealer*, now famous for the first publication, in 1925, of William Faulkner's prose. The initial issue pronounced it "high time, we believe, for some doughty clear-visioned penman to emerge from the sodden marshes of Southern literature." Hundreds have done so, and Faulkner's work has influenced seven decades of southern writing.

In 1922, a Nashville literary group called the Fugitives* announced that "a literary phase known rather euphemistically as Southern Literature has expired, like any other stream whose source is stopped up." Instead, partly because of the Fugitives themselves, the stream flowed on, and, it seems today, is unstoppable. No one could have predicted the brilliant burst of literary achievement in the South that began in the 1920s. Supplanting the romantic novelists of the postbellum Old South, the new southern fiction writers displayed an enormous diversity of interests and daring techniques.

Among the nation's great writers of the nineteenth century were southerners Edgar Allan Poe, Mark Twain, and O. Henry. With the Southern Renaissance of the 1920s, the region's writers again moved into the forefront of American literature. Faulkner and others writing before 1950—Eudora Welty, Richard Wright, Katherine Anne Porter, Robert Penn Warren, Erskine Caldwell, Carson McCullers, Andrew Lytle—made southern fiction one of the most significant movements in contemporary American writing. After World War II, southern writers including William Styron, Flannery O'Connor, Walker Percy, Reynolds Price, Ellen Douglas, Peter Taylor, and Ernest Gaines kept the renascence going. In the last decades of the twentieth century, the astonishing output by new writers has been called by some critics a second southern renaissance.

So, do you know these twentieth-century writers—what they care and write about, what fabulous characters inhabit their pages, what notions and ideas inform their stories, what books of theirs should be on your reading list? *The Southern Writers Quiz Book* can introduce you to intriguing worlds. It is also a test for those who already know much about southern literature.

These quizzes suggest the staggering variety of fascinating characters, exotic locales (of the mind as well as of the landscape), and multilayered concerns found in southern literature. No attempt has been made to seek out or to indicate unifying principles of southern writing. The quiz is an unabashed exercise in regional chauvinism. Play with it, and you, too, can become a southern writers groupie.

My thanks go to JoAnne Prichard and Charles East for suggestions and assistance and to Patti Henson for her witty illustrations.

*To begin, name the Fugitives.

The Southern Writers Quiz Book

1. On Writing

Name the southern authors who made the following remarks about writers and writing.

1. [A writer is] a dreamer and a conscious dreamer.

2. [A writer is] congenitally unable to tell the truth and that is why we call what he writes fiction.

3. [A writer is] a simple-minded person . . . He's not a great mind, he's not a great thinker, he's not a great philosopher, he's a story-teller.

4. [Writing is] a craft. You have to take your apprenticeship in it like anything else.

5. [Writing is] the product of someone's neurosis.

6. Writing seems to me to be a solitary, private, miserable business.

7. When I start writing a book I never know exactly all the things that will happen in it, but I know certain things. It's like taking a train to Louisiana; I know I'm going to go through Texas, and that I will arrive by a certain day, but I don't know how the weather is going to be, who will sit next to me, what the conductor's going to look like. These are the little details you don't know when you start writing.

8. Whatever our theme in writing, it is old and tried. Whatever our place, it has been visited by the stranger, it will never be new again. It is only the vision that can be new; but that is enough.

9. Whatever impetus I had towards writing owes nothing to sitting on a porch listening to anybody tell stories about the south, believe me . . .

10. Writing is a religion with me.

2. Opening Lines

Novels and stories written by southerners contain some memorable opening lines. Give titles for the works that begin with these sentences.

1. In Haddam, summer floats over tree-softened streets like a sweet lotion balm from a careless, languorous god, and the world falls in tune with its own mysterious anthems.

2. In sleep she knew she was in her bed, but not the bed she had lain down in a few hours since, and the room was not the same but it was a room she had known somewhere.

3. Come into my cell. Make yourself at home. Take the chair; I'll sit on the cot. No? You prefer to stand by the window? I understand. You like my little view.

4. When the rooster crowed, the moon had still not left the world but was going down on flushed cheek, one day short of the full. A long thin cloud crossed it slowly, drawing itself out like a name being called.

5. Mason City. To get there you follow Highway 58, going northeast out of the city, and it is a good highway and new. Or was new, that day we went up it.

6. The senior partner studied the resume for the hundredth time and again found nothing he disliked about Mitchell Y. McDeere, at least not on paper.

7. Sitting beside the road, watching the wagon mount the hill toward her, Lena thinks, "I have come from Alabama: a fur piece. All the way from Alabama, a-walking. A fur piece."

8. Just with his body and from inside like a snake, leaning that black motorcycle side to side, cutting in and out of the slow line of cars to get there first, staring due-north through goggles towards Mount Moriah and switching coon tails in everybody's face was Wesley Beavers . . .

9. It happened that green and crazy summer when Frankie was twelve years old.

10. Through the fence, between the curling flower spaces, I could see them hitting.

11. When I was little, I would think of ways to kill my daddy.

12. The candleflame and the image of the candleflame caught in the pierglass twisted and righted when he entered the hall and again when he shut the door.

13. "I see . . ." said the vampire thoughtfully, and slowly he walked across the room towards the window.

14. Her doctor had told Julian's mother that she must lose twenty pounds on account of her blood pressure, so on Wednesday nights Julian had to take her downtown on the bus for a reducing class at the Y.

3. Landscapes

In *Terrains of the Heart and Other Essays on Home*, Mississippian Willie Morris describes a montage of scenes in his home state. Match these titles containing elements of a southern montage with the appropriate authors.

1. *Homeplace*
2. *The Strength of Fields*
3. *Blue Rise*
4. *The Town*
5. *The Great Meadow*
6. *Horses Make a Landscape Look More Beautiful*
7. *River House*
8. *Providence Island*
9. *Wilderness*
10. *A Curtain of Green*
11. *The River to Pickle Beach*
12. *The Heart of a Distant Forest*

a. Eudora Welty
b. Calder Willingham
c. William Faulkner
d. Rebecca Hill
e. Philip Lee Williams
f. Doris Betts

g. Robert Penn Warren
h. Anne Rivers Siddons
i. Elizabeth Madox Roberts
j. Alice Walker
k. Stark Young
l. James Dickey

4. The Southern Renaissance

The year 1929 was a benchmark for southern writers. It was the high point of the early Southern Renaissance, and first books were published by three new writers, Thomas Wolfe, Erskine Caldwell, and Hamilton Basso. Others, already known, produced some of their best work in that year. Match the author's name to his or her 1929 book.

1. Ellen Glasgow
2. DuBose Heyward
3. Stark Young
4. James Branch Cabell
5. William Faulkner
6. Erskine Caldwell
7. Thomas Wolfe
8. Hamilton Basso

a. *The Bastard*
b. *River House*
c. *Look Homeward, Angel*
d. *They Stooped to Folly*
e. *Mamba's Daughters*
f. *The Way of Ecben*
g. *Relics and Angels*
h. *The Sound and the Fury* and *Sartoris*

5. Are You from Big T?

Match each author to a work either written by a Texan or set in Texas.

1. Katherine Anne Porter	a. *Home from the Hill*
2. Preston Jones	b. *The Last Picture Show*
3. Larry McMurtry	c. *The House of Breath*
4. William Goyen	d. *The Gay Place*
5. William Humphrey	e. "Noon Wine"
6. Billy Lee Brammer	f. *A Texas Trilogy*
7. Horton Foote	g. *Hold Autumn in Your Hand*
8. George Sessions Perry	h. *The Young Man from Atlanta*
9. Jim Lehrer	i. *Goodbye to a River*
10. Cormac McCarthy	j. *Texas*
11. Larry L. King	k. *Armadillos and Old Lace*
12. Kinky Friedman	l. *King Ranch*
13. James Michener	m. *White Widow*
14. John Graves	n. *Cities of the Plain*
15. Tom Lea	o. *The Whorehouse Papers*

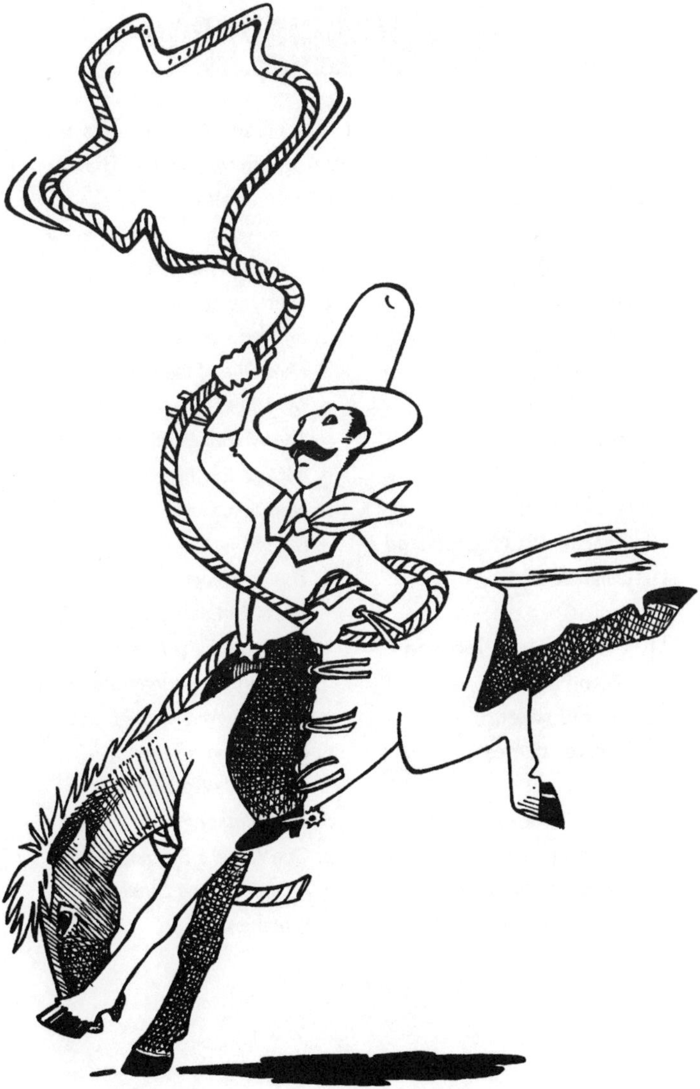

6. Autobiography

Most southern writers make rich use of autobiographical material in their fiction, and many have written nonfiction works that are clearly autobiographical. Match these writers and titles.

1. Eudora Welty
2. Andrew Lytle
3. Reynolds Price
4. Ellen Glasgow
5. Joan Williams
6. James Agee
7. Fred Chappell
8. Jesse Stuart
9. Endesha Ida Mae Holland
10. Lillian Smith

11. James Weldon Johnson
12. Lillian Hellman
13. Conrad Aiken
14. Chester Himes

15. William Alexander Percy
16. Willie Morris
17. Donald Windham
18. Clifton Taulbert

a. *A Whole New Life*
b. *Lanterns on the Levee*
c. *Emblems of Conduct*
d. *I Am One of You Forever*
e. *My Life of Absurdity*
f. *The Woman Within*
g. *A Wake for the Living*
h. *New York Days*
i. *Ushant*
j. *The Autobiography of an Ex-Colored Man*
k. *The Year of My Rebirth*
l. *Memory of a Large Christmas*
m. *From the Mississippi Delta*
n. *Once Upon a Time When We Were Colored*
o. *The Wintering*
p. *One Writer's Beginnings*
q. *A Death in the Family*
r. *Pentimento*

7. Hometowns

The much-discussed "sense of place" in southern fiction is often rooted in the author's actual hometown. Match these writers and the towns associated with them, either as their birthplaces or the places where they later lived and worked.

1. Lillian Hellman	a. Natchez, Mississippi
2. Ellen Glasgow	b. Memphis, Tennessee
3. Elizabeth Madox Roberts	c. Newport News, Virginia
4. Katherine Anne Porter	d. Oxford, Mississippi
5. Flannery O'Connor	e. Greenville, Mississippi
6. Eudora Welty	f. Cross Creek, Florida
7. Conrad Aiken	g. Savannah, Georgia
8. Kate Chopin	h. Milledgeville, Georgia
9. William Faulkner	i. Knoxville, Tennessee
10. Thomas Wolfe	j. Atlanta, Georgia
11. Marjorie Kinnan Rawlings	k. Covington, Louisiana
12. Richard Wright	l. Richmond, Virginia
13. William Styron	m. Jackson, Mississippi
14. Joan Williams	n. Yazoo City, Mississippi
15. Carson McCullers	o. Columbus, Georgia
16. Walker Percy	p. Springfield, Kentucky
17. James Agee	q. Cloutierville, Louisiana
18. Shelby Foote	r. New Orleans, Louisiana
19. James Dickey	s. Indian Creek, Texas
20. Willie Morris	t. Asheville, North Carolina

8. New Orleans

Name at least six works of fiction set in New Orleans.

9. Mountaineers

Which of the following is *not* an Appalachian writer?

Fred Chappell
Mary Lee Settle
Lee Smith
Lewis Nordan
Wilma Dykeman
David Whisnant
Jim Wayne Miller
Jesse Stuart
Harriette Arnow
James Still
Thomas Wolfe

10. Name Dropping

Can you replace the missing names of characters that appear in these titles?

1. _____ _____ *When Last Seen*, Peter Taylor
2. *Searching for* _____, Anne Tyler
3. _____*'s Choice,* William Styron
4. _____ _____*and the Miracle Man*, Fannie Flagg
5. *The Third Life of* _____ _____, Alice Walker
6. _____*by Nature*, Erskine Caldwell
7. *Mr.* _____ *and the Muses*, Gail Godwin
8. *Spence and*_____, Bobbie Ann Mason
9. *The Confessions of* _____ _____, William Styron
10. *My Dog* _____, Willie Morris
11. _____ *Speaks His Mind*, Langston Hughes
12. *Autobiography of* _____, Alex Haley
13. *The Great* _____, Pat Conroy
14. "*A Rose for* _____," William Faulkner
15. _____*'s Gourd Vine*, Zora Neale Hurston

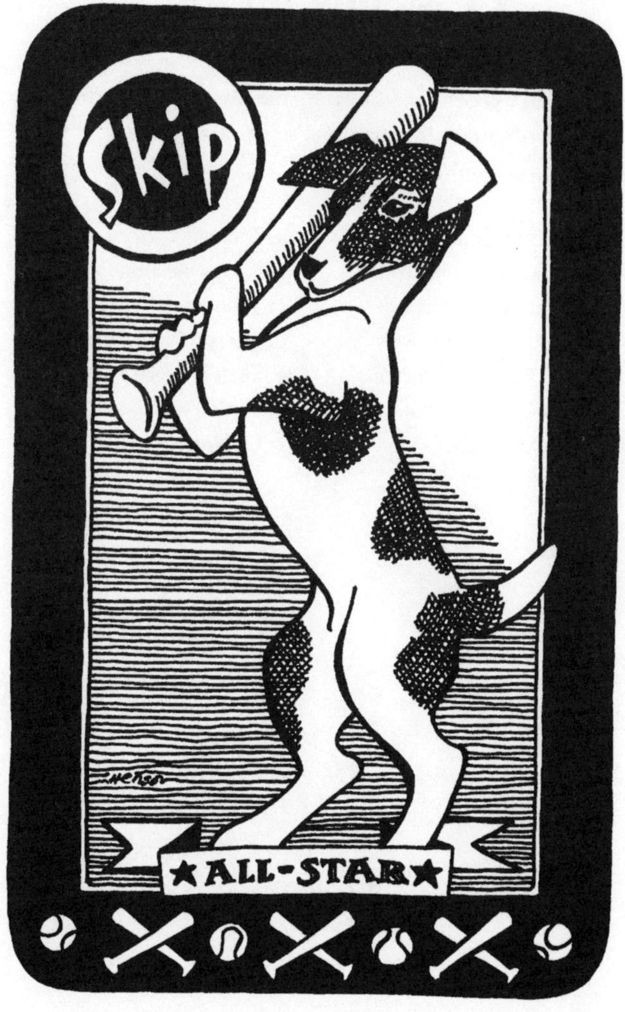
Skip
ALL-STAR

11. Noms de Plume

Some southern writers are known by names other than those they were born with or obtained through marriage. Match the real name to the one found on the book.

1. Lula Carson Smith
2. Josephine Ayres Haxton
3. Callie Russell Porter
4. Thomas Lanier Williams
5. Truman Streckfus Persons
6. William Sydney Porter
7. Samuel Clemens

a. Truman Capote
b. Katherine Anne Porter
c. Tennessee Williams
d. Carson McCullers
e. Ellen Douglas
f. Mark Twain
g. O. Henry

12. Fictional Addresses

William Faulkner's fictional Yoknapatawpha County is better known than its real counterpart, Lafayette County, Mississippi. Who created these other famous fictional addresses? Match place to author.

1. Altamont, North Carolina
2. Port Warwick, Virginia
3. Hoot Owl Holler, North Carolina
4. Beulah Valley, West Virginia
5. Eunola, Mississippi
6. Homochitto, Mississippi
7. Connemara, North Carolina
8. Redmond, Virginia
9. Morgana, Mississippi
10. Bayonne, Louisiana
11. Jordan County, Mississippi
12. Listre, North Carolina
13. Appalachee, Georgia
14. Arrow Catcher, Mississippi

a. Ellen Douglas
b. Mary Lee Settle
c. Ernest Gaines
d. Eudora Welty
e. Ellen Glasgow
f. Carl Sandburg
g. Thomas Wolfe
h. William Styron
i. Beverly Lowry
j. Lee Smith
k. Lewis Nordan
l. Raymond Andrews
m. Shelby Foote
n. Clyde Edgerton

13. Who Is Who?

Sometimes a title provides a brief and provocative description of the protagonist, with the writer then spinning a story that etches the character irrevocably in readers' minds. Match each title to a character's name. (Give yourself extra points if you know the author.)

1. *The Odd Woman*	a. Elizabeth Abbot
2. *The Sportswriter*	b. Jamie Lockhart
3. *The Optimist's Daughter*	c. Jo Spencer
4. *Oldest Living Confederate Widow Tells All*	d. Mordecai Jones
5. *The Moviegoer*	e. Sue Muffaletta
6. *Daddy's Girl*	f. Binx Bolling
7. *The Robber Bridegroom*	g. Lucy Marsden
8. *The Cheer Leader*	h. Jane Clifford
9. *The Ballad of the Flim-Flam Man*	i. Laurel McKelva
10. *The Tennis Handsome*	j. Francis Lake
11. *The Good Husband*	k. Frank Bascombe
12. *The Clock Winder*	l. French Edward

14. Almost Titles

Match each title with its earlier version.

1. *Gone with the Wind*
2. *The Sound and the Fury*
3. *The Heart Is a Lonely Hunter*
4. *The Optimist's Daughter*
5. *Lie Down in Darkness*
6. *Follow Me Down*
7. *Let Us Now Praise Famous Men*
8. "The Life You Save May Be Your Own"
9. *Look Homeward, Angel*
10. *The Wild Palms*
11. *The Glass Menagerie*
12. "The Wanderers"

a. *The Mute*
b. *Inheritance of Night*
c. *Tomorrow Is Another Day*
d. *O, Lost*
e. *The Gentleman Caller*
f. "The Hummingbirds"
g. *Twilight*
h. *Poor Eyes*

i. *Three Tenant Families*
j. *The Vortex*
k. "The World Is Almost Rotten"
l. *If I Forget Thee, Jerusalem*

15. Classic Sources

Many writers have taken titles and plots from Shakespeare's plays, the Bible, Greek myths, and other classics. Name the sources of these titles.

1. *The Sound and the Fury*, William Faulkner
2. *Something in the Wind*, Lee Smith
3. *Absalom, Absalom!*, William Faulkner
4. *Pale Horse, Pale Rider*, Katherine Anne Porter
5. *In My Father's House*, James Street
6. *Bone of My Bones*, Sylvia Wilkinson
7. *The Glory of Hera*, Caroline Gordon
8. *The Golden Apples*, Eudora Welty
9. *He Sent Forth a Raven*, Elizabeth Madox Roberts
10. *In Abraham's Bosom*, Paul Green
11. *As I Lay Dying*, William Faulkner
12. *Gather Together in My Name*, Maya Angelou
13. *Ship of Fools*, Katherine Anne Porter
14. *Let Us Now Praise Famous Men*, James Agee

16. Families

Much southern literature is concerned with family life, and the region's writers treat the subject in a variety of ways, despite Peter Taylor's title *Happy Families Are All Alike*. Match these titles and authors.

1. *The Kiss of Kin*	a. Ellen Douglas
2. *A Mother and Two Daughters*	b. Gail Godwin
3. *A Family's Affairs*	c. Alice Walker
4. *The Far Family*	d. William Goyen
5. *Kinflicks*	e. David Madden
6. *In Search of Our Mothers' Gardens*	f. Lee Smith
7. *Daddy's Girl*	g. Mary Lee Settle
8. *The Suicide's Wife*	h. Lisa Alther
9. *A Southern Family*	i. Gail Godwin
10. *The Faces of Blood Kindred*	j. Beverly Lowry
11. *Family Linen*	k. Wilma Dykeman
12. *The Brothers*	l. Frederick Barthelme

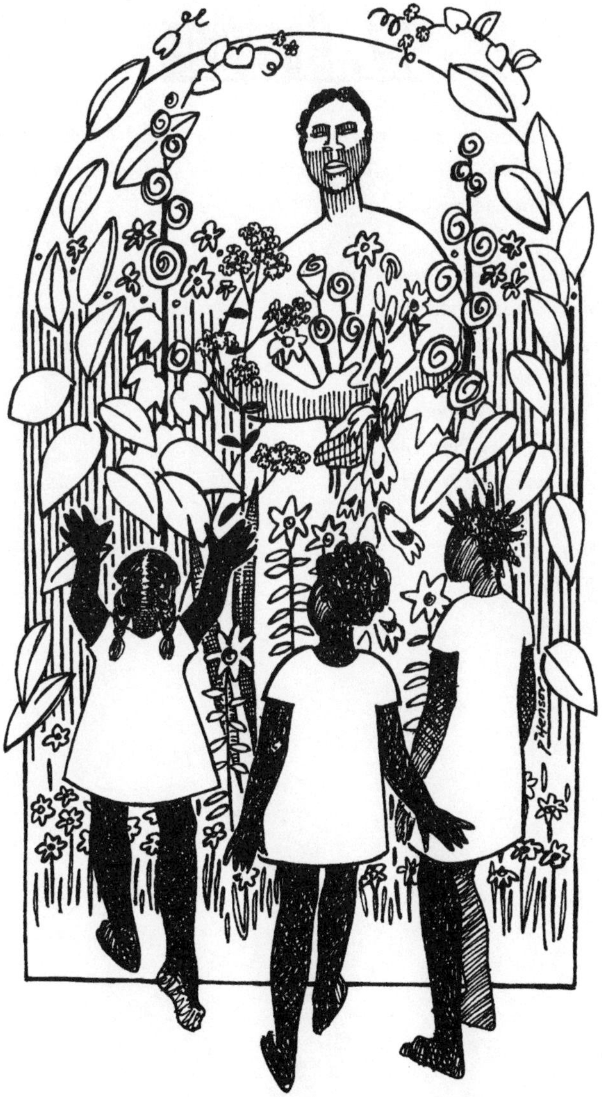
P. Henson

17. Doubling

Southern writers sometimes repeat words or use rhymes in their titles (it must be the South's musical soul). Double your pleasure by naming the authors of these works.

1. *Moonshine Light, Moonshine Bright*
2. *Black Cloud, White Cloud*
3. *Pale Horse, Pale Rider*
4. *Other Voices, Other Rooms*
5. *One Time, One Place*
6. "White Girl, Fine Girl"
7. *Our Faces, Our Words*
8. *Killer Diller*
9. *Rootie Kazootie*
10. *Rumble Tumble*

18. One Word

Brevity has been admired since Hamlet proclaimed it the soul of wit, and many southern writers appreciate the quality. Match the following authors with their one-word book titles.

1. Jayne Anne Phillips		a.	*Cane*
2. Berry Morgan		b.	*Lancelot*
3. Jean Toomer		c.	*Pylon*
4. Mary Lee Settle		d.	*Chroma*
5. Walker Percy		e.	*Roots*
6. James Dickey		f.	*Shelter*
7. William Faulkner		g.	*Prisons*
8. John Barth		h.	*Deliverance*
9. Harry Crews		i.	*Car*
10. James Branch Cabell		j.	*Pursuit*
11. Barry Hannah		k.	*Abundance*
12. Frederick Barthelme		l.	*Chimera*
13. Beth Henley		m.	*Jurgen*
14. John O. Killens		n.	*Airships*
15. Alex Haley		o.	*Tender*
16. Mark Childress		p.	*'Sippi*

19. Famous Characters

Many literary characters created by southern writers have become familiar names to readers. Can you name the works of fiction in which these appear?

1. Ignatius Reilly
2. Rosacoke Mustian
3. Stella-Rondo
4. Holly Golightly
5. Binx Bolling
6. Hannibal Lecter
7. Atticus Finch
8. Blanche DuBois
9. Scarlett O'Hara
10. Willie Stark
11. Jeeter Lester
12. Temple Drake
13. Shug Avery
14. Bigger Thomas
15. Benjy Compson

20. Close Calls

Sometimes titles chosen by southern writers are remarkably similar. Name the authors of these close calls.

1. *Deliverance* — *The Deliverance*
2. "Shiloh" — *Shiloh*
3. *Brother to a Dragonfly* — *Brother to Dragons*
4. *The Caged Birds* — *I Know Why the Caged Bird Sings*
5. *Golden Apples* — *The Golden Apples*
6. *The Innocents Abroad* — *Innocence Abroad*
7. "Rich" — *Rich in Love*
8. *Wanderers* — "The Wanderers"
9. *The Circus in the Attic* — *Toys in the Attic*
10. *Homecoming* — *Homecomings*
11. *The Cave* — *Cavedweller*
12. *Sharpshooter* — *The Sharpshooter Blues*
13. *The Bastard* — *Bastard Out of Carolina*

21. Star Attraction

Writers sometimes make a character a star by using the name as the title. Match these southern characters/titles with their authors.

1. *Kate Vaiden*
2. *Ellen Foster*
3. *Joiner*
4. *Raney*
5. *Violet Clay*
6. *Meridian*
7. *Sarah Conley*
8. *Joe*
9. *Ray*
10. *Gabriella*
11. *Cora Potts*
12. *Emma Blue*
13. *Sartoris*
14. *Gretta*
15. *Forrest Gump*

a. Winston Groom
b. William Faulkner
c. Ward Greene
d. Kaye Gibbons
e. Ellen Gilchrist
f. Gail Godwin
g. James Whitehead
h. Reynolds Price
i. Barry Hannah
j. Erskine Caldwell
k. Beverly Lowry
l. Ellen Glasgow
m. Larry Brown
n. Alice Walker
o. Clyde Edgerton

22. Historical Characters

Southern writers have sometimes used historical figures or have based characters on them. In one story, Eudora Welty brought together *three* individuals from history—John James Audubon, Lorenzo Dow, and the outlaw James Murrell. Name the historic people appearing in these novels. (Win a bonus for naming Welty's story.)

1. *All the King's Men*, Robert Penn Warren
2. *The Great Meadow*, Elizabeth Madox Roberts
3. *The Sot-Weed Factor*, John Barth
4. *None Shall Look Back*, Caroline Gordon
5. *Death of the Fox*, George Garrett
6. *At the Moon's Inn*, Andrew Lytle
7. *Sun in Capricorn*, Hamilton Basso
8. *Great Black Russian*, John O. Killens
9. *The Succession*, George Garrett
10. *Entered from the Sun*, George Garrett

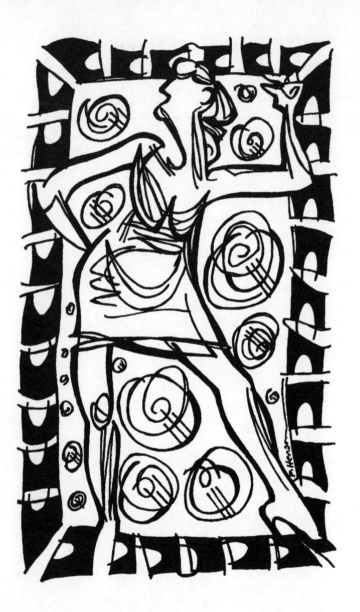

23. Women and Girls

Southern lyricist DuBose Heyward proclaimed that "woman is a some-time thing." Other southern writers have made woman an oft-time thing. Name the authors of the following works.

1. *A Woman of Means*
2. *Fair and Tender Ladies*
3. *The Odd Woman*
4. *You Can't Keep a Good Woman Down*
5. *The Women on the Porch*
6. *An Unfinished Woman*
7. *The Woman Within*
8. *A Virtuous Woman*
9. *County Woman*
10. *The Tall Woman*
11. *Goodbye, My Lady*
12. *Women with Men*
13. *The Women and the Men*
14. *I've Been a Woman*
15. *Nine Women*
16. *The Last of the Southern Girls*
17. *A Blues Book for Blue Black Magical Women*
18. *The Night of the Weeping Women*
19. *The Last Hotel for Women*
20. *Welcome to the World, Baby Girl*

24. Men and Boys

Ralph Ellison, who can be considered a marginal southerner since he was from Oklahoma, was one of America's most distinguished writers. His novel *Invisible Man*, published in 1952, has become an American classic. Match the titles of these books about men and boys with the appropriate writers.

 1. *The Old Man and the Boy*   a. Robert Penn Warren
 2. *Black Boy*   b. John A. Williams
 3. *The Last Gentleman*   c. Guy Owen
 4. *The Ballad of the Flim-Flam Man*   d. Ellen Glasgow
 5. *All the King's Men*   e. William Faulkner
 6. *The Robber Bridegroom*   f. Richard Wright
 7. *The Time of Man*   g. Ernest Gaines
 8. *Old Man*   h. Calder Willingham
 9. *The Man Who Cried I Am*   i. James Whitehead
10. *Old Powder Man*   j. Eudora Welty
11. *A Gathering of Old Men*   k. Larry Brown
12. *The Romance of a Plain Man*   l. Robert Ruark
13. *Family Men*   m. Miller Williams
14. *End as a Man*   n. Elizabeth Madox Roberts
15. *Father and Son*   o. Paul Green
16. *One Man in His Time*   p. Ellen Glasgow
17. *The Boys on Their Bony Mules*   q. Thomas Dixon, Jr.
18. *The No 'Count Boy*   r. Walker Percy
19. *The Sins of the Father*   s. John Faulkner
20. *Men Working*   t. Joan Williams
21. *Local Men*   u. Erskine Caldwell
22. *Georgia Boy*   v. Arna Bontemps
23. *Sad-Faced Boy*   w. Steve Yarbrough

25. Child Characters

Many memorable children have appeared in southern fiction. Name the writers who created these child characters.

1. Frankie Addams
2. The No Neck Monsters
3. Jody Baxter
4. Rhoda
5. Good Old Boy
6. Mick Kelly
7. Laura McRaven
8. Scout
9. Sugar
10. Child Ellen

26. Sports Heroes and Beauty Queens

Give me an A, give me a U, give me a THO, give me an R. Name the writers of these works (fiction, drama, and poetry).

1. *The Sportswriter*
2. *The Courting of Marcus Dupree*
3. *The All-Girl Football Team*
4. *The Knockout Artist*
5. *The Tennis Handsome*
6. *Fancy Strut*
7. *The Miss Firecracker Contest*
8. "The Majorette on the Self-Rising Flower Sign"
9. *Naked on Roller Skates*
10. *Karate Is a Thing of the Spirit*
11. *Aleck Maury, Sportsman*
12. *Joiner*
13. *Come Back, Lolly Ray*
14. *Jujitsu for Christ*

27. Occupations

Teachers, preachers, sharecroppers, and lawyers have played important roles in southern life, and are therefore sure to turn up in the region's fiction. Can you identify these characters by name?

1. Preacher in *The Violent Bear It Away*
2. Teacher in *Losing Battles*
3. Sharecropper in *Tobacco Road*
4. Preacher in *Light in August*
5. Lawyer in *To Kill a Mockingbird*
6. Preacher in *Wise Blood*
7. Sharecropper in *As I Lay Dying*
8. Lawyer in *The Ponder Heart*
9. Sharecropper in *God's Little Acre*
10. Lawyer in *Intruder in the Dust*

28. Courtrooms

Trial scenes appear often in southern fiction. Name novels by the following authors in which a courtroom figures prominently.

1. Harper Lee
2. William Faulkner
3. Eudora Welty
4. Robert Penn Warren
5. Jesse Hill Ford
6. Lewis Nordan
7. John Grisham

29. Angels

Celestial beings are almost as popular in southern literature as they are in that region's best-seller, the New Testament. Fill in the title that features an angel or angels by each of the following authors.

1. Elizabeth Spencer, _____ _____ _____ _____ *Angel*
2. Robert Penn Warren, _____ _____ *Angels*
3. Tennessee Williams, _____ _____ *Angels*
4. Thomas Wolfe, _____ _____, *Angel*
5. Reynolds Price, _____ _____ _____ *Angels*
6. Frank Yerby, _____ _____ _____ *Angel*
7. John Bell Clayton, _____ *Angels* _____ _____ _____
8. Hamilton Basso, _____ _____ *Angels*

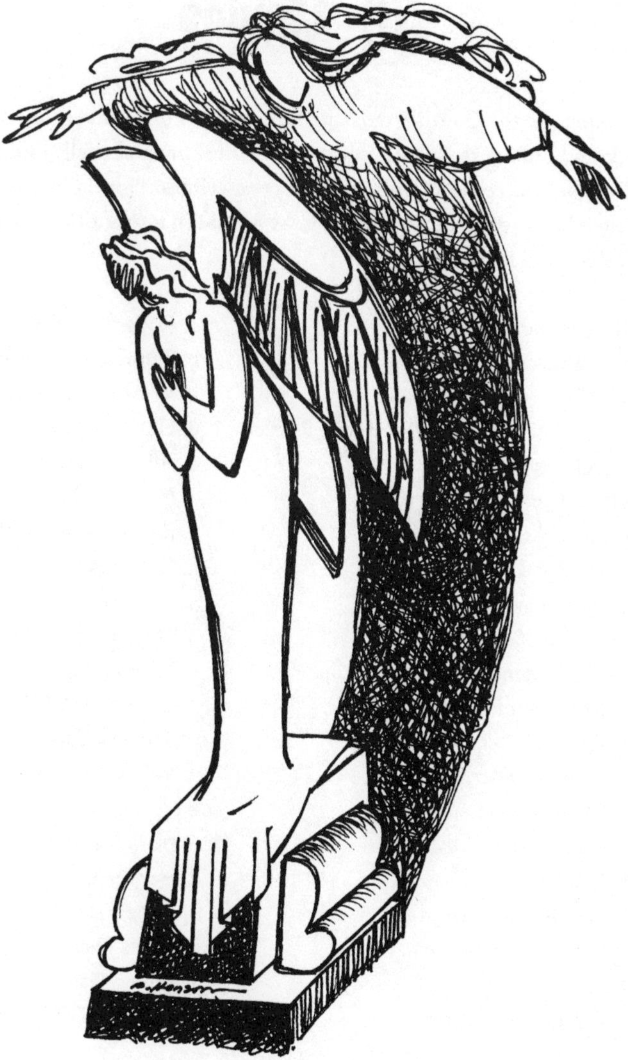

30. Movies

A number of the South's most prominent authors, including William Faulkner, Lillian Hellman, James Agee, Erskine Caldwell, and Calder Willingham, have been Hollywood screenwriters. Novels by many others have been turned into movie classics. Match movie title with author of the original book.

1. *Gone with the Wind*		a. Robert Penn Warren	
2. *The Color Purple*		b. Tennessee Williams	
3. *Ship of Fools*		c. Winston Groom	
4. *The Autobiography of Miss Jane Pittman*		d. Elizabeth Spencer	
5. *Deliverance*		e. Alice Walker	
6. *The Prince of Tides*		f. Margaret Mitchell	
7. *All the King's Men*		g. Katherine Anne Porter	
8. *The Accidental Tourist*		h. Charles Portis	
9. *Light in the Piazza*		i. Tom Wolfe	
10. *Bonfire of the Vanities*		j. Tennessee Williams	
11. *The Roman Spring of Mrs. Stone*		k. Thomas Harris	
12. *Breakfast at Tiffany's*		l. Ben Ames Williams	
13. *To Kill a Mockingbird*		m. Truman Capote	
14. *Sophie's Choice*		n. William Faulkner	
15. *The Reivers*		o. William Styron	
16. *A Streetcar Named Desire*		p. Mary Johnston	
17. *True Grit*		q. Harper Lee	
18. *Silence of the Lambs*		r. Anne Tyler	
19. *Leave Her to Heaven*		s. James Dickey	
20. *Forrest Gump*		t. Ernest Gaines	
21. *To Have and To Hold*		u. Flannery O'Connor	

22. *Fried Green Tomatoes*   v. Fannie Flagg
23. *Wise Blood*   w. Madison Jones
24. *I Walk the Line*   x. Pat Conroy

Movies per se have also been a theme in a number of titles. Name the authors of these works.

1. *The Last Picture Show*
2. *Bijou*
3. *The Moviegoer*
4. *Coming Attractions*

31. The Civil War

In 1929 Evelyn Scott wrote a huge, bold novel, *The Wave*, which still stands as the most ambitious attempt to capture in fiction the experience of the Civil War. Shelby Foote's three-volume work is the definitive study of that major event in southern history, and James Alan McPherson and Clifford Dowdey have also made important contributions in the field of nonfiction. The following writers used the Civil War as subject matter in works of fiction and poetry; match them with the correct titles (one author has two works).

1. Andrew Lytle
2. Shelby Foote
3. Clifford Dowdey
4. Stark Young
5. Robert Penn Warren
6. Allen Tate
7. Margaret Mitchell
8. Ellen Glasgow
9. Caroline Gordon
10. William Faulkner
11. Ben Ames Williams
12. T. S. Stribling
13. David Madden
14. James Street
15. James Boyd
16. Charles Frazier
17. Howard Bahr
18. Madison Jones
19. Donald Davidson

a. *Sharpshooter*
b. *None Shall Look Back*
c. *House Divided*
d. *Marching On*
e. *Bugles Blow No More*
f. *The Long Night*
g. *The Unvanquished*
h. *Gone with the Wind*
i. *So Red the Rose*
j. *The Battle-Ground*
k. *Shiloh*
l. *The Fathers*
m. *By Valour and Arms*
n. *Band of Angels*
o. *The Forge*
p. "Ode to the Confederate Dead"
q. *Nashville 1864*
r. *Cold Mountain*
s. *The Black Flower*
t. "Lee in the Mountains"

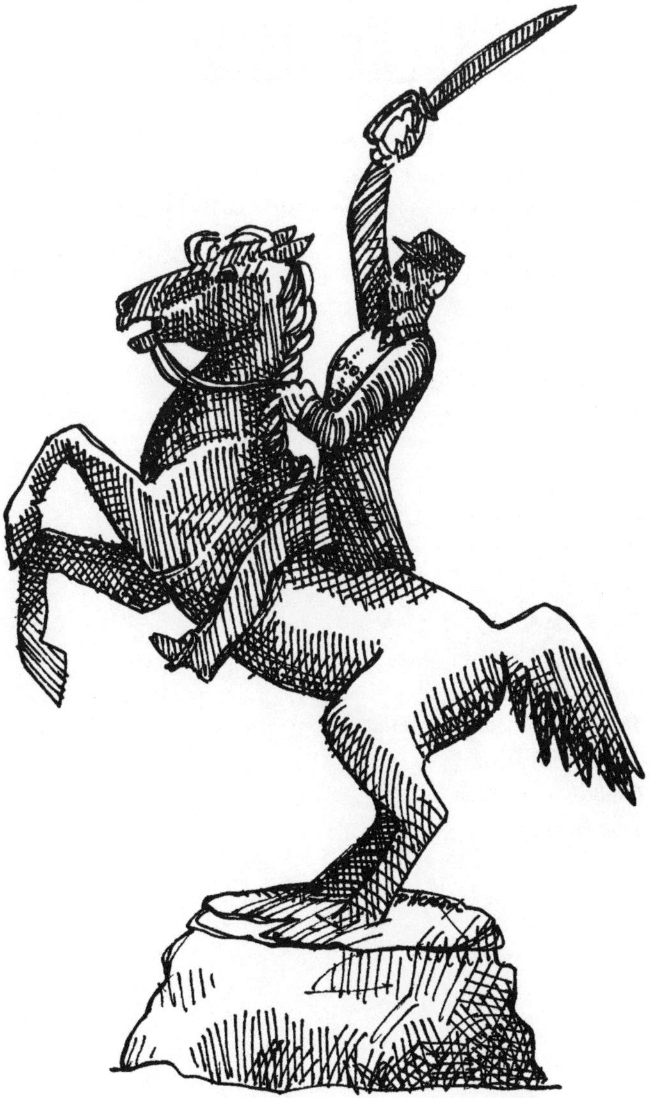

32. Broadway

Several southern writers have made it to the Great White Way, either by being dramatists themselves or by having their novels adapted for the stage by someone else. Name the author of the original work.

1. *The Ponder Heart*
2. *The Glass Menagerie*
3. *All the Way Home*
4. *The Last Meeting of the Knights of the White Magnolia*
5. *The Member of the Wedding*
6. *Look Homeward, Angel*
7. *The Rose Tattoo*
8. *Requiem for a Nun*
9. *Crimes of the Heart*
10. *Porgy*
11. *Toys in the Attic*
12. *The Grass Harp*
13. *The Trip to Bountiful*
14. *The Square Root of Wonderful*
15. *Driving Miss Daisy*
16. *The Boys in the Band*
17. *Tobacco Road*

33. Birds

Maya Angelou knows why the caged bird sings. Other southern writers have used birds on the wing as metaphors. Match these titles and authors.

1. *The Eagle's Shadow*
2. *The Eccentricities of a Nightingale*
3. *To Kill a Mockingbird*
4. *The Red Cock Crows*
5. *He Sent Forth a Raven*
6. *The Hawk Is Dying*
7. *Can't Get a Red Bird*
8. *Old Fish Hawk*
9. *The Pelican Brief*
10. *Bird of Paradise*

a. Harper Lee
b. Vicki Covington
c. Mitchell F. Jayne
d. Dorothy Scarborough
e. Tennessee Williams
f. James Branch Cabell
g. John Grisham
h. Elizabeth Madox Roberts
i. Frances Gaither
j. Harry Crews

34. Music

Music—blues, country, mainstream hymns, and gospel—floats through southern life and writing like a motif. It is not surprising that many southern writers allude to music or use fragments of lyrics in their titles. Match each music-based title to its author.

1. *The Gospel Singer*
2. *Music from Spain*
3. *Black Mountain Breakdown*
4. *Chitlin Strut and Other Madrigals*
5. *Do, Lord, Remember Me*
6. *A Little Book in C Major*
7. *O, Beulah Land*
8. *Where the Music Was: Stories*
9. *Can't Quit You, Baby*
10. *Pay the Piper*

a. Ellen Douglas
b. Charles East
c. Joan Williams
d. Harry Crews
e. Eudora Welty
f. Lawrence Wells
g. George Garrett
h. Mary Lee Settle
i. William Price Fox
j. H. L. Mencken

11. *Spin a Soft Black Song*	k. Paul Green
12. *Music of the Swamp*	l. Fred Chappell
13. *Blessed Assurance*	m. James Weldon Johnson
14. *Brighten the Corner Where You Are*	n. Allan Gurganus
15. *Facing the Music*	o. Fred Chappell
16. *Let the Band Play Dixie*	p. John A. Williams
17. *Lift Every Voice and Sing*	q. Nikki Giovanni
18. *Roll, Sweet Chariot*	r. Albert Murray
19. *!Click Song*	s. Lee Smith
20. *Farewell, I'm Bound to Leave You*	t. Larry Brown
21. *Stomping the Blues*	u. Lewis Nordan

35. Flora

"Things grow bigger in the South," says horticulturist Felder Rushing in *Gardening Southern Style*, adding that they do so profusely, in all seasons and in a variety of climates, from nearly subtropical to cool and mountainous. Flowers, trees—flora of all sorts—loom large in southern writing. Name the authors (who may or may not be gardeners) of the following works.

1. "Flowering Judas"
2. *The Bitterweed Path*
3. "A Tree of Night"
4. *A Rose for Ana Maria*
5. "Revolutionary Petunias"
6. *The Last Day the Dogbushes Bloomed*
7. *The Tin Can Tree*
8. *Among Birches*
9. *Clover*
10. *Under the Vulture Tree*
11. "Ode to the Chinaberry Tree"
12. *The Desert Rose*
13. *Heaven Trees*
14. *Rambling Rose*
15. "An Odor of Verbena"
16. *Jonah's Gourd Vine*
17. *A Curtain of Green*
18. *A Highly Ramified Tree*

36. Fauna

Creatures, large and small, creepy and calm, inhabit the pages of southern literature. The following titles might be announcements at a zoo. Match them with their authors.

1. *The Night of the Iguana*
2. *Mosquitoes*
3. *You Can't Pet a Possum*
4. *The Condor Passes*
5. *A Feast of Snakes*
6. *Mules and Men*
7. *All the Pretty Horses*
8. *The Yearling*
9. *Lamb in His Bosom*
10. *The Vixens*
11. *The Bite of the Diamond Rattler*
12. *Watch for the Fox*
13. *The Little Foxes*
14. *The Silence of the Lambs*
15. *Brother to a Dragonfly*
16. *Beasts of the Southern Wild*

a. Will Campbell
b. Zora Neale Hurston
c. Cormac McCarthy
d. Marjorie Kinnan Rawlings
e. Doris Betts
f. Tennessee Williams
g. Thomas Harris
h. Arna Bontemps
i. Lillian Hellman
j. William Goyen
k. Frank Yerby
l. Caroline Miller
m. William Mills
n. William Faulkner
o. Harry Crews
p. Shirley Ann Grau

37. Weather and Seasons

Mark Twain said that weather is "a literary specialty, and no untrained hand can turn out a good article on it." The following titles refer to weather conditions or seasons. Can you match them with the appropriate author?

1. *A Killing Frost*
2. "Blackberry Winter"
3. "Gooseberry Winter"
4. "Cotton Candy on a Rainy Day"
5. *The Wind Shifting West*
6. *The Weather Shelter*
7. *Tall Houses in Winter*
8. *Jingling in the Wind*
9. *Love in a Dry Season*
10. *The Snow Poems*
11. *On the Big Wind*
12. *And Then We Heard the Thunder*
13. *To the Winds*
14. *Lunatic Wind*

a. Elizabeth Madox Roberts
b. David Madden
c. Doris Betts
d. Nikki Giovanni
e. Bobbie Ann Mason
f. Sylvia Wilkinson
g. Erskine Caldwell
h. A. R. Ammons
i. Robert Penn Warren
j. Shirley Ann Grau
k. Shelby Foote
l. Madison Jones
m. William Price Fox
n. John Oliver Killens

38. The Land

Acknowledging the South as a rich farming area, Kentuckian Wendell Berry entitled a book of poetry *The Gift of Good Land*. As it appears in the titles of many southern works, however, the land does not sound very arable. Match these titles describing hard-scrabble conditions with the correct author.

 1. *Barren Ground*
 2. *The Hills Beyond*
 3. *A Circle of Stone*
 4. *Scorched Earth*
 5. *A Stand in the Mountains*
 6. *The Dark Mountains*
 7. *Tragic Ground*
 8. *The Rock Cried Out*
 9. *The Killing Ground*
10. *Hard Scrabble: Observations on a Patch of Land*
11. *A Buried Land*
12. *My Land Is Dying*

a. Ellen Douglas
b. Peter Taylor
c. William Hoffman
d. Madison Jones
e. Ellen Glasgow
f. Mary Lee Settle
g. Harry Caudill
h. Erskine Caldwell
i. Miller Williams
j. Thomas Wolfe

k. Stuart Stevens
l. John Graves

39. Southern Food

James Street's *The Biscuit Eater* refers to a dog, but there are plenty of enthusiastic eaters among the South's human population. While foods and references to eating appear in many titles, surprisingly few reflect the staples of southern cooking. Match these titles and authors.

1. *A Feast Made for Laughter*
2. *Dinner at the Homesick Restaurant*
3. *Fried Green Tomatoes at the Whistle Stop Cafe*
4. *Crash Diet*
5. *Double Muscadine*
6. *Red Bean Row*
7. *Crabcakes*
8. "Green Figs at Table"
9. *Spring Onions and Cornbread*
10. "Noon Wine"
11. "Still Life with Watermelon"
12. *To Eat a Peach*

a. Anne Tyler
b. Jill McCorkle
c. Bettie Sellers
d. Robert Emmet Kennedy
e. Craig Claiborne
f. Fannie Flagg
g. Katherine Anne Porter
h. James Alan McPherson
i. Bobbie Ann Mason
j. Frances Gaither
k. Conrad Aiken
l. Calder Willingham

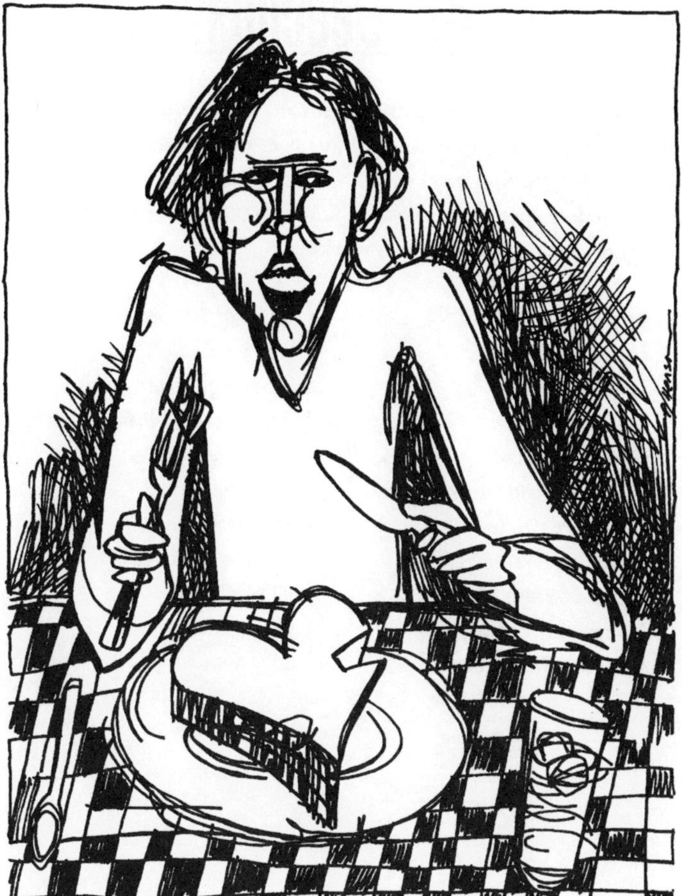

40. Beaches

For some people, imagining the South means conjuring up visions of plowed fields, tangled undergrowth, or remote mountains, and they are surprised to learn that most of the southern states have coastlines. Naturally, beaches appear in works of fiction from the region. Match titles and authors (one writer has two works).

1. *Beach Music*
2. *Ferris Beach*
3. *The Salt Line*
4. *Gulf Coast Stories*
5. *Gulf Coast Country*
6. *Ship Island and Other Stories*
7. "Gulfport"
8. *Small Craft Warnings*
9. "To the White Sea"
10. *A Tidewater Morning*
11. *A Coast of Trees: Poems*

a. William Styron
b. Lee Smith
c. Hodding Carter
d. Tennessee Williams
e. Pat Conroy
f. A. R. Ammons
g. Elizabeth Spencer
h. Erskine Caldwell
i. Jill McCorkle
j. James Dickey

41. Social Occasions

Kaye Gibbons's *On the Occasion of My Last Afternoon* does not refer to a social occasion, but many works of southern fiction do revolve around family and community events. Name the authors of the following.

1. *Cakewalk*
2. *Tennessee Day in St. Louis*
3. *Delta Wedding*
4. *Celebration*
5. *A Long Fourth*
6. *The Debutante Ball*
7. *The Light Infantry Ball*
8. *Welcome to the Arrow-Catcher Fair*
9. *Fight Night on a Sweet Saturday*
10. *The Fireman's Fair*

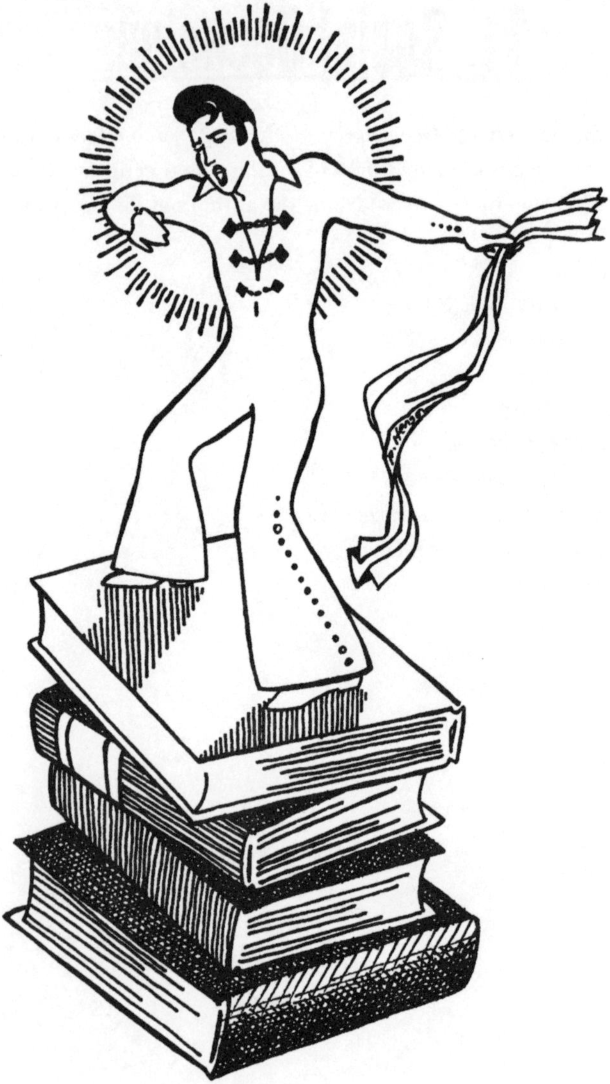

42. Love Me Tender

Elvis sang about it; southerners write about it. Do the love match and test your knowledge of these writers and their approaches to affairs of the heart. Fill in the blanks.

1. *The _____, _____ Love*, Walter Sullivan
2. *Of Love and _____*, Ernest Gaines
3. *Love in the _____*, Walker Percy
4. *Love in a _____ _____*, Shelby Foote
5. *_____ of Love*, Shirley Ann Grau
6. *The Love _____*, Mary Lee Settle
7. *Love and _____*, Reynolds Price
8. *In Love and _____*, Alice Walker
9. *"_____ in Love,"* Donald Justice
10. *_____with Love*, Ellen Gilchrist
11. *Love _____*, Bobbie Ann Mason
12. *_____ _____ Love*, Larry Brown
13. *_____ Love*, Miller Williams
14. *Love and _____*, Erskine Caldwell
15. *Love _____ the _____ a _____*, John Dufresne

43. Colors

Match these colorful titles with their authors.

1. *The Color Purple*
2. *The Hard Blue Sky*
3. *The Rose Tattoo*
4. *Reflections in a Golden Eye*
5. *The Kandy-Kolored Tangerine-Flake Streamline Baby*
6. *So Red the Rose*
7. *The Scarlet Thread*
8. *Ruby Red*
9. *Green Centuries*
10. *Black Tickets*
11. *Silver Rights*
12. *Appalachee Red*

a. Doris Betts
b. Raymond Andrews
c. Alice Walker
d. Jayne Anne Phillips

e. Constance Curry
f. Caroline Gordon
g. Tom Wolfe
h. Shirley Ann Grau
i. Carson McCullers
j. Stark Young
k. William Price Fox
l. Tennessee Williams

44. Southern Poets

Which of these writers is not a poet? (Caution: many novelists and short story writers are also poets.)

A. R. Ammons
Brooks Haxton
James Dickey
Maya Angelou
Wendell Berry
James Weldon Johnson
John Willliam Corrington
Julia Fields
Dabney Stuart
Miller Williams
Sterling Plumpp
Nikki Giovanni
Donald Justice
John Stone
James Applewhite
Richard Ford
Fred Chappell
Reynolds Price
Aleda Shirley
Gregg Miller
Bettie Sellers
Tennessee Williams
James Seay

45. Tennessee

Name the Tennessee Williams plays in which these well-known quotations appear.

1. "I have always depended on the kindness of strangers."

2. "Blow out your candles, Laura—and so good-bye . . ."

3. "I've been accused of having a death wish, but I think it's life I wish for, terribly, shamelessly, on any terms whatever."

4. "What do you know about this mendacity thing? Hell! I could write a book on it! Don't you know that? I could write a book on it and still not cover the subject."

5. "Nothing human disgusts me unless it's unkind, violent."

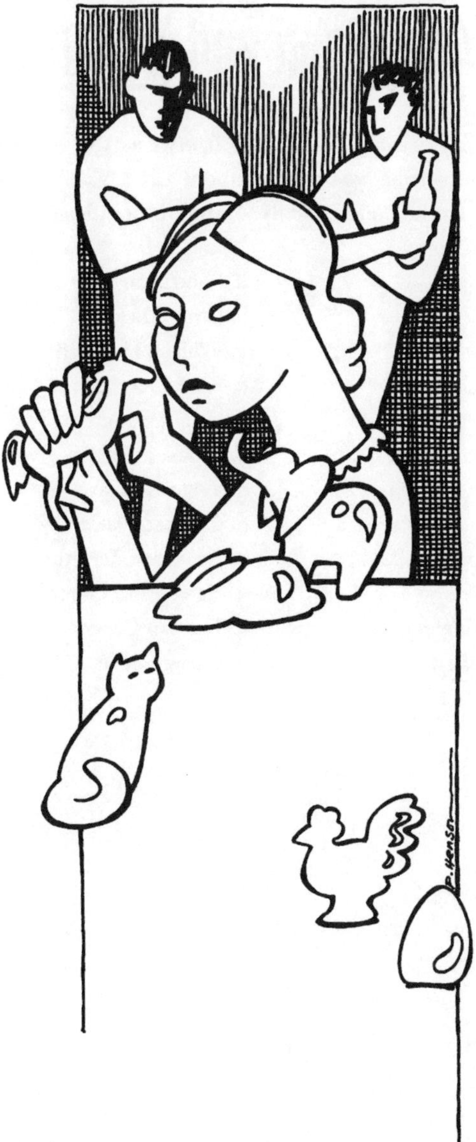
P. Henson

46. Blood and Irony

Ellen Glasgow prescribed "blood and irony" as the way to liven up southern literature. She was talking about Civil War novels, but the advice has been applied more widely. Match these titles and authors.

1. "Bloodfire"
2. *Wise Blood*
3. *Bloodline*
4. *Blood Meridian*
5. "Blood for a Stranger"
6. *Blood on the Forge*
7. *Blood Tie*
8. "Blood"
9. *In Cold Blood*
10. *Bloody Ground*
11. *Blood and Grits*
12. *Tidewater Blood*

a. Randall Jarrell
b. James Dickey
c. William Hoffman
d. Fred Chappell
e. Mary Lee Settle
f. Ernest J. Gaines
g. William Attaway
h. Cormac McCarthy
i. Fiswoode Tarleton
j. Flannery O'Connor
k. Truman Capote
l. Harry Crews

47. Religion

Calling her native region "Christ-haunted," Flannery O'Connor wrote that "[b]y and large people in the South still conceive of humanity in theological terms." To Doris Betts, that means that the southern artist must come to terms with religion. Robert Penn Warren said that *all* fiction writing has to do with the saving or loss of the immortal soul to good or evil. Match the title to the author.

1. *Souls Raised from the Dead*	a. Calder Willingham
2. *The Devil's Dream*	b. Doris Betts
3. *Ghost and Flesh*	c. Lisa Alther
4. *Their Eyes Were Watching God*	d. Berry Morgan
5. *The Mystic Adventures of Roxie Stoner*	e. Arna Bontemps
6. *Eternal Fire*	f. James Branch Cabell
7. *Original Sins*	g. Randall Kenan
8. *The Devil's Own Dear Son*	h. Carson McCullers
9. *Child of God*	i. Cormac McCarthy
10. "A Roadside Resurrection"	j. Lee Smith
11. "Revelations"	k. Larry Brown
12. *God Sends Sunday*	l. William Goyen
13. *A Visitation of Spirits*	m. Zora Neale Hurston

48. The Heavens

Mississippi-born Ben Ames Williams had great success in 1941 with the book and movie *Leave Her to Heaven*. Other southern writers have also considered the heavens. Match these titles with their authors.

1. *At Heaven's Gate*
2. *Celestial Navigation*
3. *Carolina Moon*
4. *Moon Deluxe*
5. *And Venus Is Blue*
6. *Me and My Baby View the Eclipse*
7. *The Astronomer and Other Stories*
8. *The Hard Blue Sky*
9. *Five Minutes in Heaven*
10. *Starcarbon*
11. *Trees of Heaven*
12. *Dixiana Moon*
13. *Simply Heavenly*
14. *Lasso the Moon*
15. *Comanche Moon*

a. Langston Hughes
b. Jesse Stuart
c. Mary Hood
d. Lisa Alther
e. Robert Penn Warren
f. Jill McCorkle
g. Frederick Barthelme
h. William Price Fox
i. Larry McMurtry
j. Shirley Ann Grau
k. Dennis Covington
l. Ellen Gilchrist
m. Lee Smith
n. Anne Tyler
o. Doris Betts

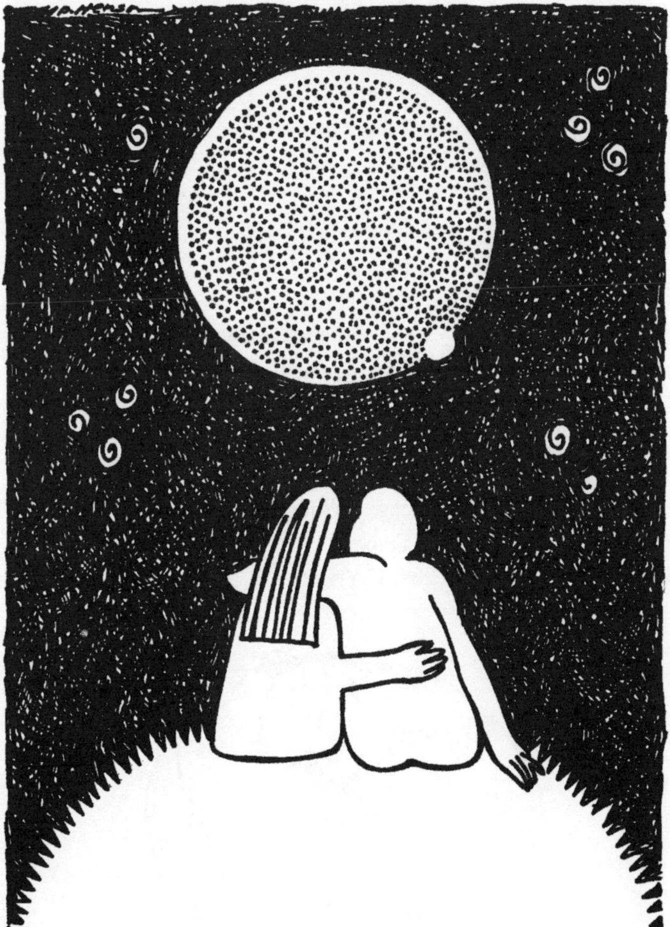

49. Dreams

Edgar Allan Poe wrote, "All that we see or seem, / Is but a dream within a dream." Southern writers since have had all manner of dreams. Fill in the missing words.

1. *Dreams of _____*, Josephine Humphreys
2. *Dream _____*, Gail Godwin
3. *_____ Dreams*, Jayne Anne Phillips
4. *_____ _____ _____ _____ Dreamy Dreams*, Ellen Gilchrist
5. *A _____ of Dreams*, William Hoffman
6. *_____ the Dreams _____*, Ellen Douglas
7. *A _____ for Dreams*, Kaye Gibbons
8. *The _____ Dream*, Lee Smith
9. "The Dream _____," Langston Hughes
10. *_____ Dreams*, Stuart Stevens
11. *The _____ Dream*, Richard Wright

72

50. Hearts

Fill in the words missing from these titles with heart.

1. *The Heart Is a _____ _____*, Carson McCullers
2. *The _____ of the Heart*, Daphne Athas
3. *_____ of the Heart*, Beth Henley
4. *The _____ Heart*, Eudora Welty
5. *The _____ in the Heart*, Hubert Creekmore
6. *A _____ of My Heart*, Richard Ford
7. *_____ Hearts*, Reynolds Price
8. *_____ Hearts*, Rita Mae Brown
9. *_____ of the Heart*, Willie Morris
10. *The Heart of a _____*, Maya Angelou
11. "*The _____ Heart*," Carson McCullers
12. *_____ of the Heart*, Elizabeth Spencer
13. *And in the _____ Heart*, Conrad Aiken
14. *My Heart and My _____*, Elizabeth Madox Roberts

51. Time

Poet Carl Sandburg, who spent some time in the South, described time as "a sandpile we run our fingers in." Southern writers have played with the sands of time, using the motif in provocative and stimulating ways. Name the authors of the following works.

1. *Scoundrel Time*
2. *Clock without Hands*
3. *One Hour*
4. *The Wheel of Life*
5. *The Clock Winder*
6. *World Enough and Time*
7. *Now Is the Time*
8. *The Year the Lights Came On*

52. Traveling

Eudora Welty's story "Death of a Traveling Salesman" is one of many southern tales that revolve around traveling. Southerners have been on the move, by foot, by mule, by train, and by car. Match the title to the author.

1. *Permit Me Voyage*
2. *All God's Children Need Traveling Shoes*
3. *Going to the Territory*
4. *The Journey*
5. *A Walk to the River*
6. *Passage Through Gehenna*
7. *Follow Me Down*
8. *Home from the Hill*
9. *In a Farther Country*
10. *Foreseeing the Journey*
11. *The Last Train North*
12. *Meet Me in the Green Glen*
13. *North Toward Home*
14. *October Journey*
15. *Heading West*
16. *Halfway from Hoxie*
17. *Gone for Good*
18. *Night Ride Home*
19. *In a U-Haul North of Damascus*
20. *The Lonesome Traveler*

a. William Humphrey
b. William Goyen
c. Miller Williams
d. Maya Angelou
e. Clifton Taulbert
f. James Applewhite
g. Madison Jones
h. Robert Penn Warren
i. William Hoffman
j. Willie Morris
k. James Agee
l. Ralph Ellison
m. Margaret Walker Alexander
n. Lillian Smith
o. Shelby Foote
p. John William Corrington
q. David Bottoms
r. Mark Childress
s. Vicki Covington
t. Doris Betts

53. Death

Death—natural, accidental, and forced—is often explored in southern fiction. Match title with author.

1. *A Death in the Family*
2. *Morgan's Passing*
3. *The Undertaker's Garland*
4. *The Wake of Jamey Foster*
5. *A Superior Death*
6. *The Suicide's Wife*
7. *Requiem for a Nun*
8. *A Time to Kill*
9. *The Optimist's Daughter*
10. *Off for the Sweet Hereafter*
11. *Crossed Over: A Murder, a Memoir*
12. *In Cold Blood*

a. Beth Henley
b. William Faulkner
c. Beverly Lowry
d. Nevada Barr
e. James Agee
f. John Peale Bishop
g. Eudora Welty
h. David Madden
i. Gail Godwin
j. John Grisham
k. Anne Tyler
l. T. R. Pearson

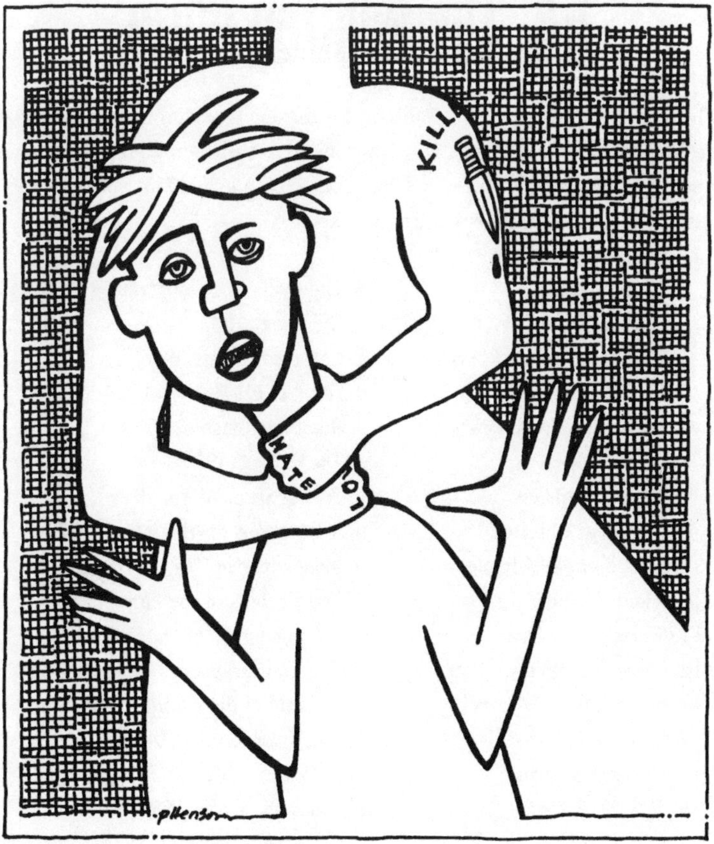
KILL
HATE

54. The Pulitzer Prize

While only one southerner, William Faulkner, has won the Nobel Prize for literature, many have won the coveted Pulitzer Prize (Faulkner won two, for *The Reivers* in 1963 and *A Fable* in 1955). Match these fiction writers with their winning works.

1. Ellen Glasgow	a. *The Optimist's Daughter*, 1973
2. Harper Lee	b. *The Store*, 1933
3. Marjorie Kinnan Rawlings	c. *Collected Stories*, 1966
4. Eudora Welty	d. *Lamb in His Bosom*, 1934
5. Katherine Anne Porter	e. *Breathing Lessons*, 1989
6. Anne Tyler	f. *The Yearling*, 1939
7. Caroline Miller	g. *Scarlet Sister Mary*, 1929
8. Margaret Mitchell	h. *A Summons to Memphis*, 1987
9. John Kennedy Toole	i. *Independence Day*, 1996
10. Alice Walker	j. *The Keepers of the House*, 1965
11. Shirley Ann Grau	k. *A Confederacy of Dunces*, 1981
12. Larry McMurtry	l. *The Confessions of Nat Turner*, 1968
13. Robert Penn Warren	m. *A Death in the Family*, 1958
14. James Agee	n. *The Color Purple*, 1983
15. William Styron	o. *In This Our Life*, 1942
16. T. S. Stribling	p. *Lonesome Dove*, 1986
17. Julia Peterkin	q. *Gone with the Wind*, 1937
18. Peter Taylor	r. *To Kill a Mockingbird*, 1961
19. Richard Ford	s. *All the King's Men*, 1947

The Pulitzer has also gone to southern dramatists and poets. Name the authors of these works.

1. *In Abraham's Bosom*, 1927
2. *A Streetcar Named Desire*, 1948
3. *Cat on a Hot Tin Roof*, 1955
4. *Crimes of the Heart*, 1981
5. *Driving Miss Daisy*, 1988
6. *The Kentucky Cycle*, 1992
7. *The Young Man from Atlanta*, 1995
8. *Selected Poems*, 1980
9. *Promises: Poems 1954–1956*, 1958
10. *Now and Then: Poems 1976–1978*, 1979

55. Cheers and Boos

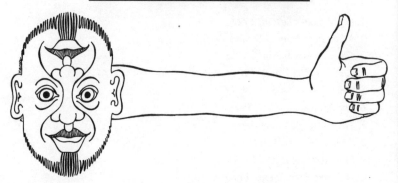

Comments made by southern writers regarding the work of other southern writers are sometimes complimentary and sometimes not. Identify the following speakers.

1. [I]n my opinion anybody that admires Thomas Wolfe can be expected to like good fiction only by accident.

2. One thing that bored the hell out of me with the late fine writer Truman Capote was that he was always making it perfectly clear what an early genius he was.

3. Even though I've gone out of my way to avoid Faulkner, in spite of my—because of my admiration, nevertheless, I find myself thinking, "Oh God, that sounds like him," you know, when I write it. Faulkner is at once the blessing and curse of all Southern novelists, maybe all novelists.

4. I admire the work of Faulkner that I know—by no means all—but with a cold, distant admiration for a genius whom I know to be grand but who has proved irrelevant to my own obsessions, my own ambitions.

5. Thomas Wolfe said, "You can't go home again," and I said, "Nonsense, that is the only place you can go. You go there all the time."

6. William Humphrey, who has just published a brilliant novel, *The Ordways*, is the only writer I know who ever said in print that his writing and his style and his feeling about writing have been influenced by me. I have read carefully everything he has published, and I cannot see a trace of my influence to save my neck. But if he wants to say I influenced him, I'm very flatttered, for I do so like what he writes.

7. Mr. Truman Capote makes me plumb sick, as does Mr. Tennessee Williams.

8. No man ever put more of his heart and soul into the written word than did William Faulkner. If you want to know all you can about that heart and soul, the fiction where he put it is still right there.

9. I certainly think Eudora Welty is the living writer that I admire most.

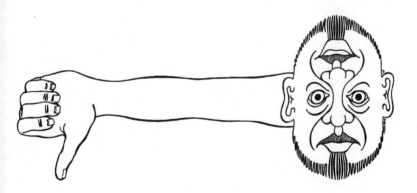

56. The Scientific South

Southern writers have used a surprising number of titles with scientific allusions. (Don't expect a book's contents to reflect the title; remember the southern penchant for metaphor.) Match the title to the author.

1. *Everything that Rises Must Converge*
2. *Light Can Be Both Wave and Particle*
3. *Sphere: The Form of a Motion*
4. *Phases of an Inferior Planet*
5. *Some Side Effects of Time Travel*
6. *Celestial Navigation*
7. *The Floatplane Notebooks*
8. *Following Gravity*

a. Ellen Glasgow
b. Clyde Edgerton
c. James Applewhite
d. Flannery O'Connor
e. Ellen Gilchrist
f. Anne Tyler
g. A. R. Ammons
h. Gail Godwin

57. Trivia

What southern writer

1. is the only person, southern or otherwise, to receive a Pulitzer Prize for both fiction and poetry (two for poetry)?

2. was a photographer whose work was shown at the Museum of Modern Art in New York?

3. attended high school in New York, and lived there most of his life?

4. battled pornography charges?

5. enlisted in the Royal Canadian Air Force?

6. became a television star on the PBS series *The Civil War*?

7. introduced the topic of lesbianism to the American stage?

8. wrote the book and lyrics for George Gershwin's opera, *Porgy and Bess*?

9. was a medical doctor?

10. writes articles and books about auto racing?

11. was the leading New York theatre critic of the 1920s?

12. grew up in a North Carolina boardinghouse called "My Old Kentucky Home"?

13. exiled himself to Paris for more than half his writing career?

14. was married to the photographer Margaret Bourke-White?

15. left instructions that her dogs Jeremy and Billy be exhumed from their graves in her backyard garden and buried with her?

16. had a goose named Clair Booth Loose Goose and five ducks whose names were Merrill, Lynch, Pierce, Fenner, and Bean?

17. appears as a character in another southern writer's novel?

18. was born in a log cabin?

19. died of a heart attack while riding in a taxi in New York City?

20. is the model for the preacher Will B. Dunn in the comic strip *Kudzu* by southern cartoonist Doug Marlette?

21. called her famous character Pansy O'Hara in early drafts of her only novel?

22. won the Pulitzer Prize the year Faulkner's masterpiece *Absalom, Absalom!* was published?

58. Intriguing Titles

Add some of your favorites or make your own list.

Divine Secrets of the Ya-Ya Sisterhood, Rebecca Wells

"Said There Was Somebody Talking to Him Through the Air Conditioner," James Seay

We a BadddDDD People, Sonia Sanchez

Truth: Four Stories I Am Finally Old Enough to Tell, Ellen Douglas

Garbage, A. R. Ammons

The Magic Striptease, George Garrett

Crazy in Alabama, Mark Childress

The Smell of Matches, John Stone

The Secret History, Donna Tartt

On the 7th Day God Created the Chevrolet, Sylvia Wilkinson

Last One Home Sleeps in the Yellow Bed, Leon Rooke

The Boo, Pat Conroy

Fast Lanes, Jayne Anne Phillips

This Thing Don't Lead to Heaven, Harry Crews

Answers

PREFACE: Members of the Fugitives were John Crowe Ransom, Donald Davidson, Allen Tate, and Robert Penn Warren.

1. ON WRITING: 1. Carson McCullers; 2. William Faulkner; 3. Erskine Caldwell; 4. Katherine Anne Porter; 5. William Styron; 6. Walker Percy; 7. Ernest Gaines; 8. Eudora Welty; 9. Walker Percy; 10. Shelby Foote.

2. OPENING LINES: 1. *Independence Day*, Richard Ford; 2. "Pale Horse, Pale Rider," Katherine Anne Porter; 3. *Lancelot*, Walker Percy; 4. *Losing Battles*, Eudora Welty; 5. *All the King's Men*, Robert Penn Warren; 6. *The Firm*, John Grisham; 7. *Light in August*, William Faulkner; 8. *A Long and Happy Life*, Reynolds Price; 9. *The Member of the Wedding*, Carson McCullers; 10. *The Sound and the Fury*, William Faulkner; 11. *Ellen Foster*, Kaye Gibbons; 12. *All the Pretty Horses*, Cormac McCarthy; 13. *Interview with the Vampire*, Anne Rice; 14. "Everything that Rises Must Converge," Flannery O'Connor.

3. LANDSCAPES: 1. Anne Rivers Siddons; 2. James Dickey; 3. Rebecca Hill; 4. William Faulkner; 5. Elizabeth Madox Roberts; 6. Alice Walker; 7. Stark Young; 8. Calder Willingham; 9. Robert Penn Warren; 10. Eudora Welty; 11. Doris Betts; 12. Philip Lee Williams.

4. THE SOUTHERN RENAISSANCE: 1. *They Stooped to Folly*; 2. *Mamba's Daughters*; 3. *River House*; 4. *The Way of Ecben*; 5. *The Sound and the Fury* and *Sartoris*; 6. *The Bastard*; 7. *Look Homeward, Angel*; 8. *Relics and Angels*.

5. ARE YOU FROM BIG T?: 1. "Noon Wine"; 2. *A Texas Trilogy*; 3. *The Last Picture Show*; 4. *The House of Breath*; 5. *Home from the Hill*; 6. *The Gay Place*; 7. *The Young Man from Atlanta*; 8. *Hold Autumn in Your Hand*; 9. *White Widow*; 10. *Cities of the Plain*; 11. *The Whorehouse Papers*; 12. *Armadillos and Old Lace*; 13. *Texas*; 14. *Goodbye to a River*; 15. *King Ranch*.

6. AUTOBIOGRAPHY: 1. *One Writer's Beginnings*; 2. *A Wake for the Living*; 3. *A Whole New Life*; 4. *The Woman Within*; 5. *The Wintering*; 6. *A Death in the Family*;

7. *I Am One of You Forever*; 8. *The Year of My Rebirth*; 9. *From the Mississippi Delta*; 10. *Memory of a Large Christmas*; 11. *The Autobiography of an Ex-Colored Man*; 12. *Pentimento*; 13. *Ushant*; 14. *My Life of Absurdity*; 15. *Lanterns on the Levee*; 16. *New York Days*; 17. *Emblems of Conduct*; 18. *Once Upon a Time When We Were Colored*.

7. HOMETOWNS: 1. New Orleans; 2. Richmond; 3. Springfield; 4. Indian Creek; 5. Milledgeville; 6. Jackson; 7. Savannah; 8. Cloutierville; 9. Oxford; 10. Asheville; 11. Cross Creek; 12. Natchez; 13. Newport News; 14. Memphis; 15. Columbus; 16. Covington; 17. Knoxville; 18. Greenville; 19. Atlanta; 20. Yazoo City.

8. NEW ORLEANS: Possible titles are Ellen Gilchrist, *In the Land of Dreamy Dreams*; Shirley Ann Grau, *The House on Coliseum Street* and *The Condor Passes*; Walker Percy, *The Moviegoer*; Hamilton Basso, *Days Before Lent*; Eudora Welty, "No Place for You, My Love" and "Purple Hat"; John Kennedy Toole, *A Confederacy of Dunces*; Sheila Bosworth, *Almost Innocent*; Anne Rice, *The Witching Hour* and *The Feast of All Saints*.

9. MOUNTAINEERS: Lewis Nordan is from the Mississippi Delta.

10. NAME DROPPING: 1. *Miss Lenora*; 2. *Caleb*; 3. *Sophie's*; 4. *Daisy Fay*; 5. *Grange Copeland*; 6. *Jenny*; 7. *Bedford*; 8. *Lila*; 9. *Nat Turner*; 10. *Skip*; 11. *Simple*; 12. *Malcolm X*; 13. *Santini*; 14. Emily; 15. *Jonah*.

11. NOMS DE PLUME: 1. Carson McCullers; 2. Ellen Douglas; 3. Katherine Anne Porter; 4. Tennessee Williams; 5. Truman Capote; 6. O. Henry; 7. Mark Twain.

12. FICTIONAL ADDRESSES: 1. Thomas Wolfe; 2. William Styron; 3. Lee Smith; 4. Mary Lee Settle; 5. Beverly Lowry; 6. Ellen Douglas; 7. Carl Sandburg; 8. Ellen Glasgow; 9. Eudora Welty; 10. Ernest Gaines; 11. Shelby Foote; 12. Clyde Edgerton; 13. Raymond Andrews; 14. Lewis Nordan.

13. WHO IS WHO?: 1. *The Odd Woman* is Jane Clifford (Gail Godwin); 2. *The Sportswriter* is Frank Bascombe (Richard Ford); 3. *The Optimist's Daughter* is Laurel McKelva (Eudora Welty); 4. *Oldest Living Confederate Widow* is Lucy Marsden (Allan Gurganus); 5. *The Moviegoer* is Binx Bolling (Walker Percy); 6. *Daddy's Girl* is Sue Muffaletta (Beverly Lowry); 7. *The Robber Bridegroom* is Jamie Lockhart (Eudora Welty); 8. *The Cheer Leader* is Jo Spencer (Jill McCorkle); 9. *The Flim-Flam Man* is Mordecai Jones (Guy Owen); 10. *The Tennis Handsome* is French Edward (Barry Hannah); 11. *The Good Husband* is Francis Lake (Gail Godwin); 12. *The Clock Winder* is Elizabeth Abbot (Anne Tyler).

14. ALMOST TITLES: 1. *Tomorrow Is Another Day*; 2. *Twilight*; 3. *The Mute*; 4. *Poor Eyes*; 5. *Inheritance of Night*; 6. *Vortex*; 7. *Three Tenant Families*; 8. "The World Is Almost Rotten"; 9. *O, Lost*; 10. *If I Forget Thee, Jerusalem*; 11. *The Gentleman Caller*; 12. "The Hummingbirds."

15. CLASSIC SOURCES: 1. *Macbeth*; 2. *A Comedy of Errors*; 3. 2 Samuel 19: 4; 4. Revelations 6: 8; 5. John 14: 2; 6. Genesis 2: 23; 7. Greek mythology; 8. Greek mythology; 9. Genesis 8: 7; 10. Luke 16: 22; 11. *The Odyssey*; 12. Matthew 18: 20; 13. *Das Narrenschiff*, Sebastian Brant; 14. the Apocrypha, Ecclesiasticus 44: 1.

16. FAMILIES: 1. Mary Lee Settle; 2. Gail Godwin; 3. Ellen Douglas; 4. Wilma Dykeman; 5. Lisa Alther; 6. Alice Walker; 7. Beverly Lowry; 8. David Madden; 9. Gail Godwin; 10. William Goyen; 11. Lee Smith; 12. Frederick Barthelme.

17. DOUBLING: 1. William Price Fox; 2. Ellen Douglas; 3. Katherine Anne Porter; 4. Truman Capote; 5. Eudora Welty; 6. Shirley Ann Grau; 7. Lillian Smith; 8. Clyde Edgerton; 9. Lawrence Naumoff; 10. Joe R. Lansdale.

18. ONE WORD: 1. *Shelter*; 2. *Pursuit*; 3. *Cane*; 4. *Prisons*; 5. *Lancelot*; 6. *Deliverance*; 7. *Pylon*; 8. *Chimera*; 9. *Car*; 10. *Jurgen*; 11. *Airships*; 12. *Chroma*; 13. *Abundance*; 14. *'Sippi*; 15. *Roots*; 16. *Tender*.

19. FAMOUS CHARACTERS: 1. *A Confederacy of Dunces*, John Kennedy Toole; 2. *A Long and Happy Life*, Reynolds Price; 3 "Why I Live at the P.O.," Eudora Welty; 4. *Breakfast at Tiffany's*, Truman Capote; 5. *The Moviegoer*, Walker Percy; 6. *Silence of the Lambs*, Thomas Harris; 7. *To Kill a Mockingbird*, Harper Lee; 8. *A Streetcar Named Desire*, Tennessee Williams; 9. *Gone with the Wind*, Margaret Mitchell; 10. *All the King's Men*, Robert Penn Warren; 11. *Tobacco Road*, Erskine Caldwell; 12. *Sanctuary*, William Faulkner; 13. *The Color Purple*, Alice Walker; 14. *Native Son*, Richard Wright; 15. *The Sound and the Fury*, William Faulkner.

20. CLOSE CALLS: 1. James Dickey and Ellen Glasgow; 2. Bobbie Ann Mason and Shelby Foote; 3. Will Campbell and Robert Penn Warren; 4. LeRoy Leatherman and Maya Angelou; 5. Marjorie Kinnan Rawlings and Eudora Welty; 6. Mark Twain and Emily Clark; 7. Ellen Gilchrist and Josephine Humphreys; 8. Mary Johnston and Eudora Welty; 9. Robert Penn Warren and Lillian Hellman; 10. Sonia Sanchez and Willie Morris; 11. Robert Penn Warren and Dorothy Allison; 12. David Madden and Lewis Nordan; 13. Erskine Caldwell and Dorothy Allison.

21. STAR ATTRACTION: 1. Reynolds Price; 2. Kaye Gibbons; 3. James Whitehead; 4. Clyde Edgerton; 5. Gail Godwin; 6. Alice Walker; 7. Ellen Gilchrist; 8. Larry Brown; 9. Barry Hannah; 10. Ellen Glasgow; 11. Ward Greene; 12. Beverly Lowry; 13. William Faulkner; 14. Erskine Caldwell; 15. Winston Groom.

22. HISTORICAL CHARACTERS: 1. Huey P. Long; 2. Daniel Boone; 3. Ebenezer Cooke; 4. Nathan Bedford Forrest; 5. Sir Walter Raleigh; 6. Hernando de Soto; 7. Huey P. Long; 8. Alexander Pushkin; 9. Elizabeth I and James I; 10. Christopher Marlowe. Welty's story is "A Still Moment."

23. WOMEN AND GIRLS: 1. Peter Taylor; 2. Lee Smith; 3. Gail Godwin; 4. Alice Walker; 5. Caroline Gordon; 6. Lillian Hellman; 7. Ellen Glasgow; 8. Kaye Gibbons; 9. Joan Williams; 10. Wilma Dykeman; 11. James Street; 12. Richard Ford; 13. Nikki Giovanni; 14. Sonia Sanchez; 15. Shirley Ann Grau; 16. Willie Morris; 17. Sonia Sanchez; 18. Lawrence Naumoff; 19. Vicki Covington; 20. Fannie Flagg.

24. MEN AND BOYS: 1. Robert Ruark; 2. Richard Wright; 3. Walker Percy; 4. Guy Owen; 5. Robert Penn Warren; 6. Eudora Welty; 7. Elizabeth Madox Roberts; 8. William Faulkner; 9. John A. Williams; 10. Joan Williams; 11. Ernest Gaines; 12. Ellen Glasgow; 13. Steve Yarbrough; 14. Calder Willingham; 15. Larry Brown; 16. Ellen Glasgow; 17. Miller Williams; 18. Paul Green; 19. Thomas Dixon, Jr.; 20. John Faulkner; 21. James Whitehead; 22. Erskine Caldwell; 23. Arna Bontemps.

25. CHILD CHARACTERS: 1. Carson McCullers; 2. Tennessee Williams;

3. Marjorie Kinnan Rawlings; 4. Ellen Gilchrist; 5. Willie Morris; 6. Carson McCullers; 7. Eudora Welty; 8. Harper Lee; 9. Lewis Nordan; 10. Frank Trippett.

26. SPORTS HEROES AND BEAUTY QUEENS: 1. Richard Ford; 2. Willie Morris; 3. Lewis Nordan; 4. Harry Crews; 5. Barry Hannah; 6. Lee Smith; 7. Beth Henley; 8. James Seay; 9. Maxwell Bodenheim; 10. Harry Crews; 11. Caroline Gordon; 12. James Whitehead; 13. Beverly Lowry; 14. Jack Butler.

27. OCCUPATIONS: 1. George Rayber or Francis Marion Tarwater; 2. Julia Mortimer; 3. Jeeter Lester; 4. Gail Hightower; 5. Atticus Finch; 6. Hazel Motes; 7. Anse Bundren; 8. Dorris R. Gladney; 9. Ty Ty Walden; 10. Gavin Stevens.

28. COURTROOMS: 1. *To Kill a Mockingbird*; 2. *Requiem for a Nun*; 3. *The Ponder Heart*; 4. *World Enough and Time*; 5. *The Liberation of Lord Byron Jones*; 6. *Wolf Whistle*; 7. *A Time to Kill*.

29. ANGELS: 1. *No Place for an Angel*; 2. *Band of Angels*; 3. *Battle of Angels*; 4. *Look Homeward, Angel*; 5. *The Tongues of Angels*; 6. *Tobias and the Angel*; 7. *Six Angels at My Back*; 8. *Relics and Angels*.

30. MOVIES: 1. Margaret Mitchell; 2. Alice Walker; 3. Katherine Anne Porter; 4. Ernest Gaines; 5. James Dickey; 6. Pat Conroy; 7. Robert Penn Warren; 8. Anne Tyler; 9. Elizabeth Spencer; 10. Tom Wolfe; 11. Tennessee Williams; 12. Truman Capote; 13. Harper Lee; 14. William Styron; 15. William Faulkner; 16. Tennessee Williams; 17. Charles Portis; 18. Thomas Harris; 19. Ben Ames Williams; 20. Winston Groom; 21. Mary Johnston; 22. Fannie Flagg; 23. Flannery O'Connor; 24. Madison Jones.

MOVIES PER SE: 1. Larry McMurtry; 2. David Madden; 3. Walker Percy; 4. Fannie Flagg.

31. THE CIVIL WAR: 1. *The Long Night*; 2. *Shiloh*; 3. *Bugles Blow No More*; 4. *So Red the Rose*; 5. *Band of Angels*; 6. *The Fathers* and "Ode to the Confederate Dead"; 7. *Gone with the Wind*; 8. *The Battle-Ground*; 9. *None Shall Look Back*; 10. *The Unvanquished*; 11. *House Divided*; 12. *The Forge*; 13. *Sharpshooter*; 14. *By Valour and Arms*; 15. *Marching On*; 16. *Cold Mountain*; 17. *The Black Flower*; 18. *Nashville 1864*; 19. "Lee in the Mountains."

32. BROADWAY: 1. Eudora Welty; 2. Tennessee Williams; 3. James Agee; 4. Preston Jones; 5. Carson McCullers; 6. Thomas Wolfe; 7. Tennessee Williams; 8. William Faulkner; 9. Beth Henley; 10. DuBose Heyward; 11. Lillian Hellman; 12. Truman Capote; 13. Horton Foote; 14. Carson McCullers; 15. Alfred Uhry; 16. Mart Crowley; 17. Erskine Caldwell.

33. BIRDS: 1. James Branch Cabell; 2. Tennessee Williams; 3. Harper Lee; 4. Frances Gaither; 5. Elizabeth Madox Roberts; 6. Harry Crews; 7. Dorothy Scarborough; 8. Mitchell F. Jayne; 9. John Grisham; 10. Vicki Covington.

34. MUSIC: 1. Harry Crews; 2. Eudora Welty; 3. Lee Smith; 4. William Price Fox; 5. George Garrett; 6. H. L. Mencken; 7. Mary Lee Settle; 8. Charles East; 9. Ellen Douglas; 10. Joan Williams; 11. Nikki Giovanni; 12. Lewis Nordan; 13. Allan Gurganus; 14. Fred Chappell; 15. Larry Brown; 16. Lawrence Wells; 17. James Weldon Johnson; 18. Paul Green; 19. John A. Williams; 20. Fred Chappell; 21. Albert Murray.

35. FLORA: 1. Katherine Anne Porter; 2. Thomas Hal Phillips; 3. Truman Capote; 4. Frank Yerby; 5. Alice Walker; 6. Lee Smith; 7. Anne Tyler; 8. Rebecca Hill; 9. Dori Sanders; 10. David Bottoms; 11. James Applewhite; 12. Larry McMurtry; 13. Stark Young; 14. Calder Willingham; 15. William Faulkner; 16. Zora Neale Hurston; 17. Eudora Welty; 18. Robert Canzoneri.

36. FAUNA: 1. Tennessee Williams; 2. William Faulkner; 3. Arna Bontemps; 4. Shirley Ann Grau; 5. Harry Crews; 6. Zora Neale Hurston; 7. Cormac McCarthy; 8. Marjorie Kinnan Rawlings; 9. Caroline Miller; 10. Frank Yerby; 11. William Goyen; 12. William Mills; 13. Lillian Hellman; 14. Thomas Harris; 15. Will Campbell; 16. Doris Betts.

37. WEATHER AND SEASONS: 1. Sylvia Wilkinson; 2. Robert Penn Warren; 3. Bobbie Ann Mason; 4. Nikki Giovanni; 5. Shirley Ann Grau; 6. Erskine Caldwell; 7. Doris Betts; 8. Elizabeth Madox Roberts; 9. Shelby Foote; 10. A. R. Ammons; 11. David Madden; 12. John Oliver Killens; 13. Madison Jones; 14. William Price Fox.

38. THE LAND: 1. Ellen Glasgow; 2. Thomas Wolfe; 3. Miller Williams; 4. Stuart Stevens; 5. Peter Taylor; 6. William Hoffman; 7. Erskine Caldwell; 8.

Ellen Douglas; 9. Mary Lee Settle; 10. John Graves; 11. Madison Jones; 12. Harry Caudill.

39. SOUTHERN FOOD: 1. Craig Claiborne; 2. Anne Tyler; 3. Fannie Flagg; 4. Jill McCorkle; 5. Frances Gaither; 6. Robert Emmet Kennedy; 7. James Alan McPherson; 8. Conrad Aiken; 9. Bettie Sellers; 10. Katherine Anne Porter; 11. Bobbie Ann Mason; 12. Calder Willingham.

40. BEACHES: 1. Pat Conroy; 2. Jill McCorkle; 3. Elizabeth Spencer; 4. Erskine Caldwell; 5. Hodding Carter; 6. Elizabeth Spencer; 7. Lee Smith; 8. Tennessee Williams; 9. James Dickey; 10. William Styron; 11. A. R. Ammons.

41. SOCIAL OCCASIONS: 1. Lee Smith; 2. Peter Taylor; 3 Eudora Welty; 4. Mary Lee Settle; 5. Peter Taylor; 6. Beth Henley; 7. Hamilton Basso; 8. Lewis Nordan; 9. Mary Lee Settle; 10. Josephine Humphreys.

42. LOVE ME TENDER: 1. *Long, Long*; 2. *Dust*; 3. *Ruins*; 4. *Dry Season*; 5. *Evidence*; 6. *Eaters*; 7. *Work*; 8. *Trouble*; 9. Women; 10. *Drunk*; 11. *Life*; 12. *Big, Bad*; 13. *Imperfect*; 14. *Money*; 15. *Warps-Mind-Little*.

43. COLORS: 1. Alice Walker; 2. Shirley Ann Grau; 3. Tennessee Williams; 4. Carson McCullers; 5. Tom Wolfe; 6. Stark Young; 7. Doris Betts; 8. William Price Fox; 9. Caroline Gordon; 10. Jayne Anne Phillips; 11. Constance Curry; 12. Raymond Andrews.

44. SOUTHERN POETS: Richard Ford is the only writer named who is not a poet.

45. TENNESSEE: 1. *A Streetcar Named Desire*; 2. *The Glass Menagerie*; 3. *Sweet Bird of Youth*; 4. *Cat on a Hot Tin Roof*; 5. *The Night of the Iguana*.

46. BLOOD AND IRONY: 1. Fred Chappell; 2. Flannery O'Connor; 3. Ernest Gaines; 4. Cormac McCarthy; 5. Randall Jarrell; 6. William Attaway; 7. Mary Lee Settle; 8. James Dickey; 9. Truman Capote; 10. Fiswoode Tarleton; 11. Harry Crews; 12. William Hoffman.

47. RELIGION: 1. Doris Betts; 2. Lee Smith; 3. William Goyen; 4. Zora Neale Hurston; 5. Berry Morgan; 6. Calder Willingham; 7. Lisa Alther; 8. James Branch Cabell; 9. Cormac McCarthy; 10. Larry Brown; 11. Carson McCullers; 12. Arna Bontemps; 13. Randall Kenan.

48.THE HEAVENS: 1. Robert Penn Warren; 2. Anne Tyler; 3. Jill McCorkle; 4. Frederick Barthelme; 5. Mary Hood; 6. Lee Smith; 7. Doris Betts; 8. Shirley Ann Grau; 9. Lisa Alther; 10. Ellen Gilchrist; 11. Jesse Stuart; 12. William Price Fox; 13. Langston Hughes; 14. Dennis Covington; 15. Larry McMurtry.

49. DREAMS: 1. *Sleep*; 2. *Children*; 3. *Machine*; 4. *In the Land of*; 5. *Death*; 6. *Where-Cross*; 7. *Cure*; 8. *Devil's*; 9. *Keeper*; 10. *Malaria*; 11. *Long*.

50. HEARTS: 1. *Lonely Hunter*; 2. *Weather*; 3. *Crimes*; 4. *Ponder*; 5. *Chain*; 6. *Piece*; 7. *Good*; 8. *High*; 9. *Terrains*, 10. *Woman*, 11. Mortgaged; 12. *Landscapes*; 13. *Human*; 14. *Flesh*.

51.TIME: 1. Lillian Hellman; 2. Carson McCullers; 3. Lillian Smith; 4. Ellen Glasgow; 5. Anne Tyler; 6. Robert Penn Warren; 7. Lillian Smith; 8. Terry Kay.

52.TRAVELING: 1. James Agee; 2. Maya Angelou; 3. Ralph Ellison; 4. Lillian Smith; 5. William Hoffman; 6. Madison Jones; 7. Shelby Foote; 8. William Humphrey; 9. William Goyen; 10. James Applewhite; 11. Clifton Taulbert; 12. Robert Penn Warren; 13. Willie Morris; 14. Margaret Walker Alexander; 15. Doris Betts; 16. Miller Williams; 17. Mark Childress; 18. Vicki Covington; 19. David Bottoms; 20. John William Corrington.

53. DEATH: 1. James Agee; 2. Anne Tyler; 3. John Peale Bishop; 4. Beth Henley; 5. Nevada Barr; 6. David Madden; 7. William Faulkner; 8. John Grisham; 9. Eudora Welty; 10. T. R. Pearson; 11. Beverly Lowry; 12. Truman Capote.

54.THE PULITZER PRIZE: 1. *In This Our Life*; 2. *To Kill a Mockingbird*; 3. *The Yearling*; 4. *The Optimist's Daughter*; 5. *The Collected Stories of Katherine Anne Porter*; 6. *Breathing Lessons*; 7. *Lamb in His Bosom*; 8. *Gone with the Wind*; 9. *A Confederacy of Dunces*; 10. *The Color Purple*; 11. *The Keepers of the House*; 12. *Lonesome Dove*; 13. *All the King's Men*; 14. *A Death in the Family*; 15. *The Confessions of Nat Turner*; 16. *The Store*; 17. *Scarlet Sister Mary*; 18. *A Summons to Memphis*; 19. *Independence Day*.

PULITZERS IN DRAMA AND POETRY: 1. Paul Green; 2. Tennessee Williams; 3. Tennessee Williams; 4. Beth Henley; 5. Alfred Uhry; 6. Robert Schenkkan; 7. Horton Foote; 8. Donald Justice; 9. Robert Penn Warren; 10. Robert Penn Warren.

55. CHEERS AND BOOS: 1. Flannery O'Connor; 2. Barry Hannah; 3. Walker Percy; 4. Reynolds Price; 5. Katherine Anne Porter; 6. Katherine Anne Porter; 7. Flannery O'Connor; 8. Eudora Welty; 9. Reynolds Price.

56. THE SCIENTIFIC SOUTH: 1. Flannery O'Connor; 2. Ellen Gilchrist; 3. A. R. Ammons; 4. Ellen Glasgow; 5. Gail Godwin; 6. Anne Tyler; 7. Clyde Edgerton; 8. James Applewhite.

57. TRIVIA: 1. Robert Penn Warren; 2. Eudora Welty; 3. Truman Capote; 4. James Branch Cabell for *Jurgen* or Erskine Caldwell for *God's Little Acre;* 5. William Faulkner; 6. Shelby Foote; 7. Lillian Hellman; 8. DuBose Heyward; 9. Walker Percy; 10. Sylvia Wilkinson; 11. Stark Young; 12. Thomas Wolfe; 13. Richard Wright; 14. Erskine Caldwell; 15. Ellen Glasgow; 16. Flannery O'Connor; 17. Truman Capote (Dill in Harper Lee's *To Kill a Mockingbird*); 18. Katherine Anne Porter; 19. James Agee; 20. Will Campbell; 21. Margaret Mitchell; 22. Margaret Mitchell.